Rocks and Rock Pools

Written by
Jill Atkins

Some rocks are big.

Some rocks aren't big. They're little.

Some rocks are sharp.

Some rocks aren't sharp. They're smooth.

You can see lots of things on the rocks and in rock pools.

If you're in luck, you might see a crab.

This crab has squeezed into a gap in the rocks.

It's cool in there. It's out of the hot sun. But look out! This crab might nip you if you get too near.

Look at this crab.

Crabs like this one do not come with shells. They have to look for a shell that fits them.

Then, when they're bigger, they have to get a bigger shell.

This crab has got a bigger dwelling. It's a tin can!

This is a limpet.
Can you see limpets in this pool?

Limpets stick to rocks. You can't get them off the rocks!

If you're in luck, you might see a starfish.

It has little suckers under its legs.

The suckers help it to grip the rocks.

Isabella is looking in a rock pool. She's seen a little fish.

She's got a net and a bucket to keep it in.

She might get the fish out of the pool. Then she'll drop it back in the pool.

Adam is exploring the rock pools. He's looking for shells.

He's collected lots of shells from this big pool.

He collected some driftwood and some little rocks too. Then he set it all out on the sand.

Do you like it?

Do you like looking in rock pools?

It's fun, isn't it?